D0729974

# JOURNEY TO FREEDOM
## Study Guide Series

# JOURNEY

## TO LIVING WITH COURAGE

### Freedom from Fear

## YMCA OF MIDDLE TENNESSEE
## SCOTT REALL

THOMAS NELSON
*Since 1798*

NASHVILLE   DALLAS   MEXICO CITY   RIO DE JANEIRO   BEIJING

© 2008 by Young Men's Christian Association of Middle Tennessee

All rights reserved. No portion of this book may be reproduced, stored in a retrieval system, or transmitted in any form or by any means—electronic, mechanical, photocopy, recording, scanning, or other—except for brief quotations in critical reviews or articles, without the prior written permission of the publisher.

Published in Nashville, Tennessee, by Thomas Nelson. Thomas Nelson is a registered trademark of Thomas Nelson, Inc.

Thomas Nelson, Inc. titles may be purchased in bulk for educational, business, fund-raising, or sales promotional use. For information, please e-mail SpecialMarkets@ThomasNelson.com.

Scripture quotations marked NKJV are taken from THE NEW KING JAMES VERSION. © 1982 by Thomas Nelson, Inc. Used by permission. All rights reserved.

Scripture quotations marked NIV are taken from HOLY BIBLE: NEW INTERNATIONAL VERSION®. ©1973, 1978, 1984 by International Bible Society. Used by permission of Zondervan Publishing House. All rights reserved.

Scripture quotations marked NCV are taken from New Century Version®. © 2005 by Thomas Nelson, Inc. Used by permission. All rights reserved.

Scripture quotations marked KJV are taken from KING JAMES VERSION.

To find a YMCA near you, please visit the following Web sites:

United States of America: www.ymca.com
Canada: www.ymca.ca
England: www.ymca.org.uk
Australia: www.ymca.org.au

Visit www.restoreymca.org for more information on Restore, a life-changing ministry of the YMCA.

ISBN 978-1-4185-0772-5

*Printed in the United States of America.*
08 09 10 11 RRD 5 4 3 2 1

# CONTENTS

In my work within recovery, I've discovered most people struggle with fear. I'm familiar myself with living a fear-based life. I believe the most important journey in life is the journey away from fear. No one should live in the grips of chronic fear, and in this book you will learn how to move from a fear-based life to a faith-based life—a life grounded in the courage and freedom only God offers.

Probably the most universal fears among people are the fears of rejection and abandonment. We fear if people knew us intimately, then they would reject us. It causes us to run our whole lives. We run *to* perfectionism. We run *from* our potential, hiding in false identities. We hide in drugs and alcohol. We hide in pornography. We hide in food and eating disorders. We hide in dysfunctional relationships and codependency. We hide so well sometimes that we can't even find ourselves. We lose touch with our emotions, eventually feeling nothing. We drift from one relationship to the next, never finding our identities or having a strong sense of self-worth. Fear restrains every element of our lives once we begin to run from a false sense of rejection.

But what I've come to realize is that fear in and of itself isn't a bad thing. It's simply a feeling, and it can actually have a positive influence on one's life. The fear of God is the beginning of wisdom. Fear of being incompetent or lacking specific skills shows us our need for others. Fear can cause us to run from something harmful. Children who have a healthy fear of their parents learn to respect them and listen to their instruction, which will ultimately keep the children safe.

Fear of negative consequences of doing something dangerous or harmful is a good thing. It helps provide boundaries to the personal values we have, keeping us from living in contradiction to what we believe. Fear can be a very healthy motivator if we're thinking about jumping from a tall building, causing us to think twice because we are afraid of heights. Fear stops us in our tracks when we think about doing stupid things.

But there is a dark side of fear that can prevent us from striving for new things and reaching our full potential. This sinister fear controls and cripples, preventing us from achieving goals. Our response to fear is paramount. This is why God gives this reminder throughout the Bible: "Do not be afraid!"

I've heard it said that a coward dies many deaths, where a courageous man dies but once. This has been true in my life. I've allowed fear to prevent me from achieving success in the past. Sadly, it didn't have to be that way. And with God's help, you can face your fears, courageously work through them, and begin to live in freedom.

As I have inventoried my life, I realize the extent of the impact fear has had. Nothing else comes close. Fear dominated my existence, my choices, and my decisions. When I was a child, I had bad nightmares. I would wake up terrified and couldn't go back to sleep. I was afraid of the dark because I heard strange noises that terrified me. I was afraid of death and the dangers of living in an evil world. As I grew older, I became insecure, fearing that I wouldn't be smart enough or good enough. I feared my peers would reject me. Early in life I developed different ways to control my fears. These defense mechanisms would eventually become deeply rooted addictions in my life.

I wouldn't be alive now had I not met God and gone through a recovery process about twelve years ago. This is when God began working in my life, banishing my fears and altering my response to them. A therapist once asked me, "If you're not acting out of your addictions anymore, then why does it still hurt? Why is there still pain at the core?"

What I discovered was that even though I wasn't displaying symptoms of fear, deep down I still felt I wasn't good enough. I felt inadequate as a man. I was a poser, fearing my exposure as an incredibly flawed human being was imminent. The fear of being known and judged, and then coming up short, terrified me. But slowly, over time and with the help of wonderful people, I was able to establish a new foundational voice in my life, making the transition I pray all of you who read this may discover.

The definition of courage isn't a life absent of fear. Rather, it is doing what you are afraid of doing despite the presence of fear. One of the fundamental skills of recovery is learning to implement the principle of replacement. When we abandon our negative stifling responses to fears and replace them with courageous responses, we live life to the fullest.

In the movie *A Beautiful Mind*, Russell Crowe's character experiences severe hallucinations due to schizophrenia. Eventually, he is able to make tremendous strides toward living a relatively normal life because of the great support of the people who love him. He comes to realize his disease will always be present, but he learns to recognize and then ignore his hallucinations, preventing them from interfering with his life. This, in essence, is the purpose of this book: to take an honest look at our fears, to acknowledge them, and to walk forward with courage, altering our responses to them.

When we embrace fear, we acknowledge the struggle to live in a world where we have the responsibility to make choices. We all live with the knowledge that we're going to die, that death is imminent. How we respond to fear will determine the freedom and joy we experience in living. In the film *The Shawshank Redemption*, the character Red, played by Morgan Freeman, is released from prison—a place that has been his home for most of his life. Things were manageable in the big house, and now that he's free, he is afraid. There is a scene where we hear his inner dialogue: "It's a terrible thing to live in fear. I just want to get back to where things make sense." Red had seen just about every kind of violence and evil in his many years of incarceration. And yet he would rather live in that literal prison than be a prisoner to his internal fears in the free world. What a powerful statement about the profound effect of fear!

In our journeys to freedom, we face our fears. We need to explore and ponder them. We need to open up and reveal them to God and other supportive individuals. When we speak openly about them, we'll be able to move forward and learn to live in faith. This faith-based life will give us the courage to live as free men and women. Self-liberation is our goal. Our hope is to free ourselves from the negative grip of fear-based lives, walking as liberated men and women who are no longer controlled by fear, but who are living courageously in the freedom that God promises.

## CHAPTER ONE

# THE FEAR-BASED LIFE

*Fear takes many forms—dread, worry, panic, anxiety, self-consciousness, superstition, and negativity—and manifests itself in many ways—avoidance, procrastination, judgment, control, agitation, and perfectionism, to name just a few. Fear is our constant companion. It haunts us day and night and prevents us from living to our potential. Whether we are afraid of the dark or of being alone, failure or commitment, public speaking or flying, fear dominates our lives, affecting nearly every decision we make.*

—THOM RUTLEDGE, from *Embracing Fear and Finding the Courage to Live Your Life*

Fear can destroy the spirit and sap the energy out of our daily existence. It causes us to withdraw from the adventure of life. It stifles our creativity, because we fear the unknown. We stop dreaming, believing, reaching, loving, and ultimately, living.

Fear drives us to seek control of our entire existence, which ultimately makes life spin further out of control. In his book *The Voice of the Heart: A Call to Full Living*, Dr. Chip Dodd writes that fear brings us strength and allows us to experience risk and dependency. Ultimately, it makes us realize we need help. But if we perceive fear as a weakness we will likely respond to it with our own efforts to control our lives and every challenge that comes our way.[1]

Dodd discusses the positive aspects of fear: It can help us recognize our need for help—and where we find help, we can also find great opportunity. It makes our hearts vulnerable to trust others for assistance. Fear can help us depend upon others for skill, making us willing to work with others for mutual gain. If we express fear truthfully, we can gain wisdom.

"Unfortunately too many of us answer to fear by silencing its voice. We run from risk, eliminate trust, hide our dependency, and become fretful and controlling about collaboration. Fear offers the opportunity to trust God and others for our need for help. Or it entices us to stay stuck and destruct in self will."[2]

## WHAT ARE WE SO AFRAID OF?

In *Journey to Freedom,* we discussed four key fears that we struggle with as human beings: 1) fear of death, 2) fear of responsibility, 3) fear of isolation, and 4) the fear of meaninglessness.

Philosopher William James once said, "We lead lives inferior to ourselves, lives that don't reflect our real ability. One reason we do this is because it is more comfortable not to try hard, but life is, or should be, a struggle. Comfort should make us uncomfortable, contentment should make us discontent."[3] What James is alluding to is our easy acceptance of mediocrity. We accept poor effort, and accept lives that are safe. We become content with something far less than what we are capable of. The core reason for this is usually fear. We are afraid to try to be more, to seek more, to reach for more.

## Craig's Story

Craig Lamb is a single man in his forties who has lived in fear for most of his life. From a very young age, Craig hid in his fears and crippling insecurities, and these began self-sabotaging patterns.

"My biggest fear in life stems from being an only child, and having two parents who really didn't nurture me or fill my love tank. So I've always been afraid of being alone. Now I'm forty-seven years old and single, and I'm afraid of having no one to share my life with. I've only recently started to realize that there is somebody in my life who cares, and that's Jesus Christ. But up until now, it's been a constant struggle."

Craig's fears began in childhood:

"My earliest recollections of my fear are from when I was very young. My mother couldn't drive, so she couldn't take me to other kids' houses to play games and hang out. So I would find myself alone in my room, having to be imaginative and fantasize about things I would do if I was out with my friends. I think that was the beginning of my fear and my codependency on relationships in general. Because I had spent so much time alone, I didn't have the social skills to make friends, so I started playing sports.

"When I got my drivers license, it was like I had been set free from a dark cave, and I was literally on the road all the time. When I started playing sports, it boosted my self-esteem, but even then, I didn't know how to choose the right relationships. So I began a pattern of just being with anyone who came along, so that I wouldn't have to be alone. I didn't recognize or realize that at the time, because I didn't know how to."

I cannot tell you how terrified I once was of public speaking! Looking back, it wasn't the speaking in front of people that scared me—it was the fear of rejection and the anxiety that accompanied it. My heart would pound, my breath would get short, and I couldn't remember what I wanted to say. In the beginning, I was just like Moses who said to God, "Please, Lord, I have never been a skilled speaker. Even now, after talking to you, I cannot speak well. I speak slowly and can't find the best words" (Ex. 4:10

NCV). When I started down a career path where I knew I'd have to give public speeches, I was terrified. But I felt God had called me into a ministry of
public speaking, and I had a choice to make. Would I play it safe or accept
the adventure God had prepared for me? I decided to take the risk. And
that's the way God works; He wants us to confront our fears.

Two principles that go hand in hand with fear are freedom and
responsibility. If I am free and moving toward becoming all I can be,
then it produces new responsibilities in my life. You've often heard
that some people are afraid of success. Maybe that's a foreign concept
to you, but it's something I experienced firsthand when I was the well-
ness director at the Green Hills YMCA in Nashville, Tennessee. I was
going through a time of adjustment. I had more responsibility, which
seemed to equal more stress. I struggled with anxiety, panic attacks,
and depression over the expectations of my job. I was afraid to tackle
new challenges, so I settled in and began to only take on tasks in which
I was sure I could succeed. I wasn't about to take any risks or rock the
boat. I stopped dreaming. And in essence, once we stop dreaming and
striving, we stop living.

By nature, I am a very passionate person. I wanted more from my life,
even while in a deep state of depression. I wanted to feel, but fear drove
me inward into my own personal prison where I didn't risk anything so I
couldn't fail. As God stirred my heart and I worked through my recovery,
He began to call me forward to living again, to risking and embracing my
fears. At that point, I had to make a decision—the most monumental
decision of my life, actually. Should I leave my job? I could've easily
coasted for the next ten to fifteen years and then retired. But I listened to
God's calling to move forward; that's when I started Restore Ministries.

At that time, I had no idea *how* I was going to follow God's call. I only
knew it was my heart's cry to do something significant for His kingdom.
So I quit my job after ten years and started Restore Ministries. I had no
marketing plan, no strategy. No one had gone before me and forged a
path through the unknown. I was stepping out in faith with great
courage, facing my fears and following a path that seemed full of risk.

But by taking this enormous step, I overcame my fear of success. I even learned how to be a public speaker (my greatest terror), and I learned to lead other people, another great fear I harbored.

Another common worry we all face is the fear of being alone. If we enter into relationships from a place of fear (that is when we are "needy"), then we are operating out of our weaknesses and not our strengths. We see this at Restore Ministries all too frequently. People struggle with the fear of loneliness, rejection, and abandonment. They seek a relationship to fill the void. But when we enter into a relationship in this state of weakness and need, we settle on any relationship—no matter how inappropriate or what the consequences may be. Anyone who feels they *need* to be in a relationship, based on their fear of being alone, probably isn't ready to be in one.

Just as prevalent as the fear of being alone is the fear of intimacy, of being known at the core of our beings. This catchy phrase provides a fitting definition of intimacy: "Into me, you see." Fear is the ultimate enemy of intimacy. Our fear of being known stems from our struggles with deep feelings of inadequacy and shame. This inner conflict causes us to wear a mask, preventing others from knowing us at a deeper level. We are afraid if others really knew us, they would reject us. We don't risk vulnerability, so we keep relationships at a superficial level, never allowing others to see our true selves.

A common reaction to fear is the development of a false self, which leads us to operate out of pretenses. We do this by wearing different masks and portraying different personalities to fit the various roles we play in life. We wear different masks around our families, our coworkers, our church members, and even our friends. We carefully choose the mask that gains approval in any given situation. Putting on masks is an attempt to control our fear of rejection.

In one of our *Journey to Freedom* groups a successful dentist—who was making a million dollars a year—told of how fear had cornered him once. He said it led him to all sorts of dysfunctional attachments. As he sat with tears falling down his face, he told us how fear made him feel inadequate.

He never felt like he measured up to the standards he'd set for himself. He shared how his alcoholic father had abandoned him, which steeled his resolve to never be like his father. Instead, he became the "hero child." But the hero child is not driven by courage and faith, but by fear. The hero child fights the fear of becoming like the parent that failed them, working tirelessly to break free from this shadow. This man felt if he could outperform his father, then he could control the chaos and pain of his world. Yet in his mid-forties, and despite being successful in his career, his world crumbled and he sought release from this burden in alcohol. He couldn't maintain the energy it took to pursue perfection. Fear had driven him into addiction, and now those who loved him didn't feel loved by him. Through a discovery process, he came to understand that what he sought most was intimacy. He was longing for intimacy with his wife, with his children, and with his staff. But fear had crippled his relationships.

This brings us to the fear of love, which might seem a bit strange. Who fears love, you ask? Don't we all desire to love and to be loved? But many of us actually have a fear of loving or being loved. We fear God and others will not love us, or will eventually reject us, so we try to escape the pain of that desire for love. Maybe you have been hurt so much in your quest for love that the very thought of loving or trying to love again seems too much of a risk. So you feel that the safest thing to do is to pull back and never take a chance on love again—and, therefore, never experience the pain that might come with it.

I had a puppy when I was in my twenties, the first pet I'd had as an adult. I loved it, and it loved me—with the pure, seemingly unconditional love that only "man's best friend" can give. Then the worse thing possible happened: my dog got off his leash and was killed. It devastated me. Immense pain and sadness overcame me. When I buried the puppy, I buried the pain, vowing never to love a dog again. But then I read something by C. S. Lewis that changed my way of thinking. His words reminded me that there is risk in the pursuit of love. And if we retreat in fear and do not pursue love and desire, then we close our hearts and have nothing left to live for.

Love is a risk whether you are giving it or receiving it. Give love and there's the risk of having it rejected. Receive love and risk having it taken away. Even loving a pet involves risk. And where there's risk, there is the possibility of pain. But as the saying goes, "It is better to have loved and lost, than to have never loved at all."

A line of one of my favorite songs, "Try to Remember" by Tom Jones, says, "Without a hurt, the heart is hollow." Loving, living—a heart that is beating with passion is alive! Where there is passion, there is courage. But where there is passion, there is also suffering. In the history of humanity, what greater example of love is there than Jesus Christ going to the cross and dying a painful, humiliating death because he loved us so much? There has never been a human being who lived as courageously and so fully as Christ did. His life is the model we should live to imitate. He had fears, yes, but He boldly went ahead, knowing the cross was before Him, knowing it was going to be the toughest thing any human would face. (But He would overcome!) He lived from passion and courage, and He suffered for it. He fulfilled His destiny despite His fears! Are you living this way?

## CYNICISM: LIVING IN CHRONIC FEAR

Beyond being skeptical, cynicism serves as a defense mechanism when we are overwhelmed with fear. We fear things won't work out, so why get hopeful? While a skeptic might say, "I'm not sure this is going to work out," a cynic would say, "These things never work out!"

The definition of *cynicism* is "distrusting or disparaging the motives of others; showing the discontent of others' actions; holding a low opinion of mankind."[4] The cynic has a general disbelief in life itself. This pessimistic attitude is more or less a habitual disposition. If you constantly look on the dark side of things and believe the worst will happen, you are in danger of nurturing cynicism.

Cynicism is a lethal and toxic weapon to fight off fear, because it leads its victim to a state of hopelessness. When you lose your belief in the goodness of anything—the good will of people or God's inherent goodness—you have little reason to hope. Even worse, if you become cynical toward yourself, you're in danger of entering into a serious depressed state.

The greatest need for transformation in my own life was overcoming cynicism. I'd lost hope in everything I valued or trusted in. At my deepest core I told myself, "Scott, there is nothing good in you. Nothing is going to come from your life. God could not possibly love someone as horrible as you." I became cynical about myself and my motives and, ultimately, about God's love for me. That's a dangerous road to go down, for if we become cynical toward God, we are denying His truth about grace. If God doesn't love us, and His grace can't save us, then why did Jesus go to the Cross?

Our response to fear is *everything*! It means the difference between becoming hopeless or hopeful. Believing we can control our fear—on our own, without the help of God or a support system—is what drives our addictions and our lives. We won't feel serenity until we do the hard work of silencing our fears.

## WHAT IT MEANS TO TRY

Although he lost many elections before he made it to the White House, Abraham Lincoln eventually became one of our nation's greatest presidents. One might argue this was *because of*, rather than *despite*, his failures. Even though he was acutely aware of the apprehension about how he handled the Civil War, he fearlessly followed his own brand of leadership. He worked tirelessly and never gave up. He never stopped confronting his fears.

I love this quote by Teddy Roosevelt:

It's the man in the ring, the critic stands on the side and chips away at you, but it's the guy who is covered with sweat and blood that is trying, that is fighting the fight. It is not the critic who counts; not the man who points out how the strong man stumbles, or where the doer of deeds could have done them better. The credit belongs to the man who is actually in the arena, whose face is marred by dust and sweat and blood; who strives valiantly; who errs, who comes short again and again, because there is no effort without error and shortcoming; but who does actually strive to do the deeds; who knows great enthusiasms, the great devotions; who spends himself in a worthy cause; who at the best knows in the end the triumph of high achievement, and who at the worst, if he fails, at least fails while daring greatly, so that his place shall never be with those cold and timid souls who neither know victory nor defeat."[5]

Courageous people try; they strive, they take risks, and they are vulnerable. Life was meant to be an adventure—not a cynical journey through a world of pessimistic drought. Don't be fearful. Be an Abraham Lincoln.

When Jim Burke became the head of a new products division at Johnson & Johnson, one of his first projects was the development of a children's chest rub. The product failed miserably, and Burke was sure he'd lose his job. When he was called in to see the chairman of the board, however, he was met by a surprising reception. "Are you the one who just cost us all that money?" asked Robert Wood Johnson. "Well, I just want to congratulate you. If you are making mistakes, that means you are taking risks, and we won't grow unless you take risks." Some years later, when Burke himself became chairman of Johnson & Johnson, he loved to tell this story to young employees of the company.[6] The upside of risk is that it leads us to growth.

Often fear saps our passions. It steals the zeal to live fully, to embrace the challenges life presents. When we fear, we retreat—both backward and inward. We give up and stop growing. In order to live our lives to the fullest, we need to be motivated by the pursuit of our ultimate selves. Motivation keeps us moving forward despite our fears. Strive to persevere and live courageously and fully, embracing each day as a gift.

## REFLECTION QUESTIONS

How do you define *fear?*

Do you experience fear in your life? If so, what are some of those fears? List them below. If not, are you willing to consider the possibility that you may have, in fact, "silenced fear's voice"? If so, how?

In the fears you have listed above, what is it about these things that particularly scares you? Be specific.

Can you remember the first time you felt fear? What caused you fear as a child?

What fears have you carried into the present? How have they robbed you of living your life to the fullest?

What is something that you would really like to try, but can never envision yourself actually doing? How could you take a risk and try one of these opportunities anyway?

## REFLECTIONS

## REFLECTIONS

## CHAPTER TWO

# OUR RESPONSE TO FEAR

*God called out, "Adam where are you?" What he is
really saying, "Adam, where are you in your heart? Why
have you moved away from me? Where are you? What is
going on in you? Why have you pulled away from me?"*

— DR. CHIP DODD

## OUR RESPONSE: ISOLATION

If we go back to the beginning of human life, to Adam and Eve, we can discover the initial human response to fear in Genesis 3:10. Adam said to
God, "I heard you walking in the garden, and I was afraid because I was
naked, so I hid" (NCV). Adam and Eve disobeyed God and were afraid of
being caught, so they hid. They isolated themselves from His presence.

When we are afraid of being exposed, or when we are caught doing
something wrong, our tendency is to run and hide. This is a perfect
example of living a fear-based life. We are so afraid of rejection by man
that we hide from life. We isolate. It doesn't matter if we are in a home
or a church full of loved ones, we can still isolate ourselves from those
closest to us. Think about it; are you guilty of this isolation? You can isolate through addictions, eating disorders, or even in your work. You can
isolate in perfectionism or through fantasy. You can isolate through

rage, keeping people away. There are so many different ways that we "hide" from others. At the root of all this isolation is fear.

Over the last eight years at Restore Ministries, I have worked with many men who have struggled with sex addiction. They are classic examples of this isolation phenomenon. As they say in SA (Sex Addicts Anonymous), people with sex addictions have intimacy disorders. Because of this fear they retreat into a secret world of pornography. They cannot be intimate.

## OUR RESPONSE: RAGE

Rage happens when a deeply insecure individual reacts to fear with profoundly intense anger. In response to what may feel like uncontrollable emotions, the individual channels these emotions into fury in an attempt to control the situation. We treat rage at Restore Ministries like any other addiction; it is an addictive response to feelings and can be a life-controlling issue. If it isn't addressed, rage can become a habitual pattern of response to critical situations. People who rage are deeply insecure, and this behavior is among the most destructive we see. Rage is unleashed on others, usually those closest to the offender. The consequences are devastating. When a person is raging, what they are really saying is "I am scared."

Rage, like any other addiction, becomes a coping mechanism. It "helps" the individual deal with his or her problems in a negative way. But there's a difference between rage and anger. Anger is a normal, healthy, God-given feeling. (Even Jesus got angry.) When there is injustice in the world, it is normal and appropriate to express anger.

Dr. Chip Dodd, in his book *The Voice of the Heart*, writes:

In truth anger is probably the most important feeling we experience as emotional and spiritual human beings. Because it is the first step to authentic living. It shows our yearning and hunger for life. Anger helps us pursue full life by exposing the substance, desires and commitments of our hearts. Anger also works to enhance relationships by building bridges of intimacy with others. You know who you are in relationship with, their desires, their transparency and authenticity.[1]

Rage is not anger. It is an addictive response to control the things a person is insecure about or afraid of. Anger, on the other hand, is an expression of the heart's deepest desires and passions. The strong feelings we harbor can often be expressed in anger. When Jesus went into the temple, he was angry at the injustice and abuse that was taking place in God's house (John 2:15). Evil men were using the temple for their own greedy gain. Jesus was upset, and He expressed His anger by clearing the moneychangers from the temple.

Jesus was not raging. What if He had felt this injustice, but never did a thing about it? He would have denied what He knew was right, failing to take a stand. Anger is a healthy and normal emotion that can lead to righting the injustices of the world. We all know that it feels good to vent and, when kept under control, it's not a bad response. But rage is the complete opposite. It's not about injustice or venting. It's not about being vulnerable or showing how you feel inside. Rage is all about control.

When I was a young boy, I learned to turn my rage inward. If I came into contact with anyone who was angry with me, I would retreat inward and become afraid. Early in my life I developed this pattern of response to other people's anger. As a result, I buried my passions and ran to addictions, destroying relationships and nearly killing myself in the process. If not for the miraculous saving grace of Jesus Christ, I am confident that I would not be alive now.

## OUR RESPONSE: ANXIETY

Anxiety is a chronic state of fearfulness. At Restore, we write down all the things we are afraid of, and we physically lay the piece of paper down at the cross. If we hold on to fear, we become fear-based beings who are anxious, obsessive worry-warts. This amount of stress can lead to an early grave. (A little stress can be good—prompting us to action—but for the most part it is extremely destructive.)

Some of the people we work with have constant anxiety attacks. Their bodies are stressed beyond reason. If you put too much current through a fuse, it blows the fuse. Likewise, our bodies can overload with anxiety and fear. I know it sounds simple, but the first defense against anxiety and fear is admitting you are powerless, offering your cares to God, letting Him take them. We will tell you how to do this in the next chapter.

## OUR RESPONSE: CODEPENDENCY

Codependency has become a prominent topic at Restore Ministries, and in our culture in general. In our groups, we have seen that the classic codependent takes care of others and their problems at their own jeopardy. If they can control other people's lives, they feel they can stop fretting over their own. They enmesh themselves in other people's problems and begin the process of "fixing" them. They are addicted or dependent on how other people are doing. When they can control others, they feel that their own lives are under control.

Codependency is a no-win situation, because you simply cannot control others. Just attempting to control someone else can cause your own life to spin out of control. A perfect illustration is a wife who is married to an alcoholic. He is an addict, and she is dependent on taking care of him. She becomes a co-addict, and thus becomes codependent on him.

In her book, *Codependent No More*, Melody Beattie writes, "Codependency is many things. It is a dependency on people—on their moods, behaviors, sickness, or well-being. It is a paradoxal dependency. Codependents appear to be depended upon, but they are dependent.

They look strong, but feel helpless. They appear controlling, but in reality, are controlled themselves."[2]

At the heart of the codependent is dependency on others. Their search for happiness, fulfillment, joy, and love comes from outside of themselves. I believe that they are driven by fear: fear of not being good enough, fear of rejection, fear of abandonment. The codependent is desperately looking for someone or something to become attached to in some way, even if the attachment is dysfunctional or destructive. It gives a sense of meaning to their lives. Codependents crave companionship. Without it, they feel empty and hopeless. Their hope comes only from attachments and relationships.

Codependents are terrified of being abandoned, even if they feel trapped in a relationship. They often stay in toxic relationships because they are addicted to them. The love that they desperately long for eludes them, yet they settle and remain attached. What a codependent doesn't understand is that when you're dependent on another person or thing for your own happiness, there is no love in that relationship. Love cannot grow in the context of fear; it can only grow in an environment of freedom. Fear and control suffocate love. As 1 John 4:18 states, "God's perfect love drives out fear" (NCV). The two cannot co-exist.

## Craig's Story

Craig Lamb's greatest fear has always been of being alone, of being isolated, and this fear of being alone will lead many people into a dependency on relationships to fill the "hole in the soul." Craig said, "I simply had a desire to fill my void in my soul with a relationship, with a woman."

"The way I responded to fear was by jumping into relationships without really assessing if they were going to be toxic or healthy. I just wanted to feel secure and know that part of my life would be filled and there wouldn't be a void there—and that's very destructive when you don't look at the front end whether a person is going to be compatible with you, or whether they're a Christian or even believe in God."

Craig had not discovered his security in Christ—had not yet seen the man that God saw in him. So he was looking to women to tell him who he was. When Craig went through the *Journey to Freedom* workbook, he found the wisdom he had been seeking: "In the past, this destructive fear has caused me to get stuck in these unhealthy relationships—I just got deeper and deeper into them. And this did nothing but perpetuate the turmoil, depression, and codependency. And then, when one of these relationships would finally crash, I'd be a total wreck."

## OUR RESPONSE: HOPELESSNESS

Dr. William Mayer is a US Army chief psychiatrist who did a study on American prisoners of war held captive during the North Korean War. He found that American soldiers who had been detained were not actually treated poorly. They had adequate food, water, and shelter and were not tortured. In fact, the prisoners indicated that the physical abuse they experienced was less than any of the other prison camps known throughout history. Surprisingly, however, they had the highest death rate—38 percent—in US military history. "Even more astounding was that half of these soldiers died because they had given up. They had surrendered both mentally and physically." Dr. Mayer had discovered what he called a new disease: *extreme hopelessness.*[3] There is nothing more dangerous to the human life than hopelessness. Take away our propensity to love and be loved, and we will feel it every time.

In his book *Man's Search for Meaning*, Dr. Viktor Frankl describes something similar he experienced while in the prison camps in World War II. The Nazis stripped the prisoners of every personal belonging. The guards understood that if the prisoners could connect to a memory, they would find some sort of love or purpose and, in turn, the will to live. But when the prisoners became hopeless, and their connection to loved ones was severed, their desire to live was gone, and they would soon die.

The bottom line is that we are all born with a God-given desire to love and be loved. And God is the one foundational source of love that we must connect with if we are going to live to an abundant life. We cannot allow our hearts to be captured by the sinister hopelessness of addictions. The journey to freedom takes us from a place of fear to a place of faith in Christ.

## OUR RESPONSE: NORMALITY

Normality is accepting our human condition as "normal," despite addictions or destructive patterns in our lives. Dr. Gerald May, in *Addiction and Grace,* describes this condition of normality as being who we are. Even if one's life is destructive or dysfunctional, the individual clings to it because it's what the person knows best. The fear of stepping outside of that normality ignites a very painful process of detachment.[4] So how do you get free?

Again we find that at the heart of the struggle is fear. We are afraid to let go of the comfortable, the familiar. We resist change, even when it is good for us. Some of us know we need to lose weight, stop smoking, or sever a dysfunctional relationship, but we continue in our destructive patterns because it is normality. Fear forms a powerful cement, keeping us stuck in denial. Normality is where we settle, clinging to the destructive habits, attachments, and addictions that we're accustomed to. Fear drives us inward, and life remains the same.

How does one begin to move out of these destructive patterns? Thom Rutledge talks about this process in his book *Embracing Fear and Finding the Courage to Live Your Life.* He says fear gains its strength from our retreat. We call this a phobia. When we are afraid to do something, we avoid it. The more we avoid it, the more ingrained the fear becomes. We can apply this same idea to normality. The longer I practice an addictive behavior, the harder it is to change—because it has become my "normal." The longer I use drugs and alcohol, the greater the struggle to free me from its clutches. When our lives have been built upon addiction, we fear everything might come crashing down if we alter our behavior.

Rutledge uses an acronym for fear: Facing, Exploring, Accepting, and Responding.[5] When we face what we are afraid of, explore its origins and effects, and then accept it for what it is, we will then be able to respond appropriately. If we walk away, fear increases. But the path to freedom passes through our fears. God told Abraham, "Abram, don't be afraid. I will defend you, and I will give you a great reward" (Gen. 15:1 NCV). We find this echoed in Psalm 23: "Even if I walk through a very dark valley, I will not be afraid, because you are with me. Your rod and your shepherd's staff comfort me" (v. 4 NCV). It doesn't say we should sprint through the valley, as if death chases us. No, we can walk through the valley without fear.

This is a lesson I know well because I have been a fear-based person for most of my life. I avoided everything that scared me. And as the years went by, those fears grew in number and intensity. Probably my greatest fear was public speaking. I wouldn't sleep for a week if I knew I had to give a five-minute presentation. I was afraid of being exposed as an idiot. I was afraid even if I only had to introduce myself to a large group of people. Now, I speak publicly all over the country to large groups on a regular basis. And every time I do, I am reminded of how God helped me overcome my fear. How did I change? I just did it. As Eleanor Roosevelt once said, "You must do the thing you think you cannot do."

My friend, Dr. Baker, is a great speech coach. She told me that my fear was okay and taught me how to use it in a positive way. Fear brings a heightened awareness, which can actually be an ally rather than an enemy. Dr. Baker told me I just had to keep speaking publicly. That was one of the greatest transitions for me! I would not be where I am today without that advice, and I would've missed out on some amazing experiences.

Another weapon in dealing with fear is having the support of others. As

I mentioned, I sought the help of Dr. Baker, and I also joined a small group where I began to talk openly about my fears. These "safe" people were the support team that encouraged me and walked through my fears with me. It was a tremendous help to have others holding me up and helping me face my fears. Instinctively, one of the normal responses to fear is to become isolated because we don't want others to know what we are afraid of. But talking about one's fears ultimately helps diminish their strength.

## OUR RESPONSE: SETTLING

In my recovery work, I frequently see how fear drives people to settle for an immediate fix of something they want or need. These needs are usually very normal and important—needs such as love, closeness, intimacy, touch, affirmation, and so forth. It's human nature to go for the quick fix—the immediate, convenient remedy for our situation. That's the instant gratification mentality of our society. If we have a headache or a stomachache, we want the fastest-working medicine. If we want to buy something but don't have the cash, we use our credit card. We want what we want and we want it now. We live in a microwave society; we're only willing to wait a couple of minutes for any given solution.

This sense of immediacy becomes dangerous when fear is attached. When we're in a place if discomfort, we settle for the instant gratification or immediate medication that often becomes an addiction. When we are motivated by need, we settle. My friend Angela Thompson, a wonderful therapist, told me, "We give up what we long for, for what we need right now."

A woman in our program at Restore Ministries is in a dysfunctional relationship. And although she hates it, she remains in it. She is dependent on another person to fill her loneliness. She is settling for a disastrous relationship because she is afraid of being alone. And don't we all do the same thing? We let fear drive us to settle for things that are not good for us. We take the immediate fix to escape being in a difficult place.

As we discussed in *Journey to Freedom*, the best way to deal with fear is to face them head-on in the midst of our difficult situations. As we begin to move from a fear-based life to a faith-based life, vision motivates our faith. We can become the kind of people we want to be, living passionately in the face of fear.

When vision motivates us, we cultivate relationships that support our vision, rather than wallowing in our desperation. A person with vision understands that there is purpose in being alone with God. He doesn't need a relationship to survive. She doesn't need a drink or a bag of Twinkies to be fulfilled. It takes courage to allow yourself to be alone and feel the emptiness. But I know from experience that it is far more destructive to act out of an addictive response, trying to fill the hole that only God can fill. If you get nothing else out of this book, I pray that you get this message: Settling makes you fall for false gods. You can't put a Band-Aid over a gaping wound and expect it to heal.

In the Bible, the woman at the well who spoke with Jesus is a great example of someone settling out of need (John 4:1–26). When Jesus encounters her, He confronts her about the dysfunctional relationships in her life. She'd been married five times and was living with a man who was not her husband. Jesus told her the well water would never quench the thirst that only He could satisfy.

The woman at the well was stuck in a pattern of settling for bad men and dysfunctional relationships. In recovery, we have a word for doing things repeatedly but expecting different results: insanity. Christ invited this woman to drink of His water, so that she might not settle again for dysfunctional men. The same offer stands for us. If we run to Him, we will never need to settle because He is all we need.

## FEAR OF FAILURE

The fear of failure emerged in my life after the death of my childhood dream: to be a professional football player. I have always loved sports, and had dreamed of a career in athletics. And I was fortunate enough to actually have the talent needed to entertain those dreams.

I excelled in football and was a devoted fan of the Cleveland Browns. Having played football throughout my life, my dream was to become a professional player. But that didn't happen. I graduated from college and no pro team wanted me. I even went to a free agent tryout for the Browns and was shot down again. Then the USFL started, and I got another free agent camp tryout. Strike three (to mix my sports metaphors). These failures shot the dream down forever.

Looking back, the primary struggle of my life centered on the loss of this childhood dream. When it failed, I didn't choose a new dream. Instead, I held on to my failure, regurgitating it constantly. I replayed the scenes in my mind and thought about the things I should have done differently. When a dream doesn't become a reality, it's hard to let go—but we must! And we must move on. The key to progress in life is returning to the present and formulating new dreams.

One of the most common and destructive patterns I've seen over years of working with people is how they handle the loss of dreams. People who have had past failures, people who have had dreams go awry, often become leery of dreaming again. They lose their passion for dreaming; they can't see beyond the disappointment of previous dreams. Proverbs 29:18 (KJV) says that without a dream, the people will perish. Taking away the ability to dream is the fastest way to empty a heart of its will to live. Dreams are the very heartbeat of life! They stimulate passion, offering purpose and meaning that goes beyond carving out an everyday existence.

Looking at the power of dreams from a perspective of fear, it's easy to see where many of us struggle. We stop dreaming because we fear failure, but failure is an inevitable part of life. Thomas Edison failed countless times before he invented the light bulb, but he never quit dreaming. Odds are, the majority of our dreams will *not* work. But we learn from them and we go forward with new dreams.

After years of struggling with addictions, I got better and began my work at the YMCA. But my job at the Y didn't tap my potential. The job was safe, and I was bored and unhappy. I had settled—content to stay in the status quo because the job was easy. Then God began to work in my heart and gave me a new dream. When we let go and place ourselves in His hands, He places a new dream in our heart.

The dream God placed in my heart was the vision for Restore Ministries. This vision presented me with the difficult decision of pursuing my dream or continuing to play it safe. That was seven years ago, and God has blessed my endeavors at every turn. He brought others alongside me to push the dream further. I'm writing books now, and Restore Ministries has a national presence in YMCAs across the country. But I had to overcome my fear of failure and bring myself to the present. I had to give up the childhood dream and embrace a new dream. Many times I wanted to give up and quit, to go back to the safe job. But as I persevered, God kept coming alongside me, and as He did, the dream began to grow. I'm confident that God will give you a vision for your own life—a new dream—if you're willing to let go of the old. Leave the wasteland of failed dreams and begin afresh. Dream again.

## REFLECTION QUESTIONS

What are some of the negative ways that you respond to fear? Why?

How can you change those negative responses to healthy responses?

How do you respond to anxiety in your life? How do you counteract the stress?

What do you think is your most common pattern of response when fear creeps into your life?

What is a "normal" dysfunctional pattern that has become a way of life for you? Why do you think you might be afraid to change that pattern?

## REFLECTIONS

REFLECTIONS

## CHAPTER THREE

# THE POWER TO OVERCOME OUR FEARS

*I have told you these things, so that in me you may*
*have peace. In this world you will have trouble.*
*But take heart! I have overcome the world.*

JOHN 16:33 NIV

## THE DARK NIGHT OF THE SOUL

The phrase "dark night of the soul" is reserved for the desperate nights of our lives—times when we confront serious illness or life-changing situations. It is in these moments when a crisis, either spiritual, physical, or mental, reveals our deepest fear. It could be deep doubt, emptiness, loneliness, depression, or extraordinary loss that leaves us in a moment of desperation. In these "dark nights" our fears provide the greatest opportunities for growth, if we can overcome them. John Powell, author of *A Reason to Live! A Reason to Die!*, writes "The forks in the road of human life that demand decisions of us are always crossroads of danger and opportunity."[1]

The fundamental task in the dark night of the soul is overcoming our fears and doubt. Max Lucado writes, "Faith is a desperate dive out of the sinking boat of human effort and a prayer that God will be there to pull us out of the water."[2] But too often, we doubt and fear that God won't be there when we jump, and that keeps us stuck in a sinking boat. Doubt is the strongest urge we must fight during the dark night of the soul. It's easy to succumb to doubt when you've given all you have with no sign of change. But you must realize that all your struggling and trying is only futile human effort. The apostle Paul writes that the Lord spoke these words to him: "My grace is enough for you. When you are weak, my power is made perfect in you" (2 Cor. 12:9 NCV). Paul goes on to write, "So I am very happy to brag about my weaknesses. Then Christ's power can live in me."

As a society, we are afraid of our own weaknesses and flaws. Instead of embracing them and learning to be dependent on God, we learn self-sufficiency. But when we embrace our weaknesses and admit we can't make it alone, we can begin to trust and allow God to handle our problems—to trust that God knows us better than we know ourselves, and has since before we were born. In Psalm 139:12–16, the psalmist declares God's ultimate plan for our lives: "you knit me together in my mother's womb.... Your eyes saw my unformed body. All the days ordained for me were written in your book before one of them came to be" (NIV).

There's no dark night of the soul that God cannot see through. He will find you when you cry out to Him. So talk with him about your fears and be honest about your doubts. This talk-therapy of prayer is a way of releasing repressed fear. Speech has a way of releasing us from fear, if we speak it to the One who controls the universe.

## Craig's Story

Craig learned of his own powerlessness through means that he would never have chosen. He says: "Everything was going great for me—I was going to church, dating this wonderful woman, my job was great—and then things started slipping away. I found myself obsessed with wanting to be accepted by my girlfriend when things weren't right. We probably shouldn't have even been together—nevertheless, I went into deeper codependency with her. Then, it happened: she broke up with me when we were on the way to getting very seriously involved. And then, *on the same day*, I was forced to make a big career decision that would have taken me away from my hometown and my nine-year-old son.

"So here I was, I had lost my would-have-been fiancé—you know, in midlife, when I thought we were going to finish our lives out together married—and I had a huge decision to make as far as my job. If I said no, I was going to lose my job. And so my world was completely turned *upside down* in one week. It was rough. Both of those things together just completely tore me down. The two things that formed my life—work and a woman—had brought me down so hard that I had trouble functioning."

But God didn't leave Craig in that place very long. Because of his turmoil, he was now prepped and ready to learn how to turn his fear over the healthy way, the way that God intended. Christ's work was only just beginning.

## EMBRACING OUR POWERLESSNESS

Before we can truly understand how to overcome our fears, we have to arrive at a place of powerlessness. We have to believe that we sometimes have no control over certain situations in our lives. The admission of powerlessness is the only step we must perfect, because it allows God to become the central power in our lives. We give Him the opportunity to work in us and through us by giving up control of ourselves.

I've stated that one definition of *addiction* is control, so powerlessness, conversely, would be the antidote for overcoming addiction. It is the key to healing in recovery, because powerlessness drives us into the hands of God and leads us to serenity. If I admit that I am powerless, that I can't stop obsessing, then I can detach myself and begin to heal and find peace. The twelve-step journey is about serenity. God wants us to make peace with Him, ourselves, and with others. And then He wants us to pass that peace along.

When I got into a twelve-step program and admitted I was powerless over my addictions, God began to stabilize me. The greatest gift God gave me during my recovery was a loving, intimate relationship with Him, and it became a model for all other relationships in my life. Up to that point, I'd used people to help me deal with the emptiness in my life. I ran to relationships to medicate my pain. Like the woman at the well, I met Christ and He offered me the gift of intimacy, of being known and being who I was created to be. I was able to see that being myself was enough and rejection would not kill me.

When Christ became the central part of my life, I was able to enter other relationships from this model of strength instead of fear. I discovered freedom must always exist in our hearts and relationships for true intimacy to take place. And I had to find that intimacy with Christ before I could find it anywhere else.

### GUIDANCE

As we have discussed extensively, a common response to fear is to control. Control can take on many forms in our lives. It can be addictions, dependencies, or attachments; it can be substances, sex, food, relationships, or performance. Whatever we use to control our fears usually ends up controlling us. In my own personal recovery, what made the difference was working through the twelve steps in Mike O'Neil's book *Power to Choose*. Reading his book helped me finally recognize how I was living a fear-based life. Then I started identifying the things I was using to control my life. These things had become addictions that were controlling me. My life was spinning out of control.

In going through the first three steps of the twelve steps, I made an immediate change of direction. These first steps move you away from self-sufficiency and control to a place of being guided by God. This introduces a whole new way of living. In the first step of the journey, we admit that we are powerless over our lives, our addictions, controlling issues, and our fears. In the second step, we come to believe that the power greater than ourselves can restore us back to sanity. In step three, we make a decision to turn our will and our lives over to the care of God.

Now let's look at what God does with us. Since we have already admitted that we don't have the power to control anything, we come to understand our need for God. Only He can fill the void in our lives. Once we understand this, we can surrender all to Him, turning our lives over to His will and care. This is a total paradigm shift from how we live our lives, especially for how I had been living mine.

So I began this process of living a life of faith and being guided by God in every aspect of my life. The first place God led me into was the dark night of the soul. In *Addiction and Grace,* Dr. May refers to this as *spaciousness.* Spaciousness is when all the props that we once used to control our lives are no longer there. It is just us and God—our barren soul facing off with what our lives have become. In the dark night of the soul, we have this stark confrontation with the truth, and we see how we've become dependent on control mechanisms to get through life. We might see how afraid we are and how much faith we lack. Personally, I saw that I had not been living a faith-based life. I had not been trusting in the guidance of a powerful hand to lead me through the pitfalls of life. I was living a life totally dependent on my own resources. I was in a fast sinking boat that had once felt safe, but not anymore. I took the dive out of the boat of human effort and found that God was there to catch me.

When we travel through the dark night of the soul, we find ourselves alone with God and facing two paths—one toward life and one toward death. We can either choose to live a life of freedom or a life of bondage to our addictions.

## THE HEART AWAKENED

Only the awakened heart knows the path out of the darkness. Only the awakened heart can take His hand, go with Him, and confront the fear. In this alone time with God, He reveals to us what our addictions and distractions are.

In the movie *The Lion King*, King Mufasa poses this question to his young son, Simba: "Have you forgotten who you are?" This happened to me in the dark night of the soul when I realized I was addicted to women. Looking back, as far back as I can remember, I have needed affirmation from women. The need to feel approved and accepted by others was so important, and the need to please females was paramount because of my insecurities. More importantly, I wanted the girls to notice me. Whether it was in my activities or showing off in athletics, I was always trying to get attention from females. I was empty and the only thing that seemed to temporarily fill the emptiness was being romantically involved with a woman. When I was lonely or sad or bored, I sought female companionship to fill that emptiness. Women were my medication for the insecurities in my life. When I passed through my dark night of the soul with God, one of the first things that I had to deal with was my lust. My emptiness and loneliness was obvious, and I had always sought comfort outside of myself. I wanted distractions that would provide a mood-altering affect, but all they really provided was more insanity. I was looking for somebody to tell me I was okay, that I was loveable. And one woman was never enough; it was truly a full-blown addiction. I went from one girl to the next because my thirst was never quenched.

Because of the dependency I had for women, God kept me alone for several years so that I could depend on Him exclusively. I use to lie on the floor, crying and begging Him for a partner in life, but He knew what I really needed was Him. When I finally realized this, my heart began its awakening. A dream and a destiny began to grow inside me. Before this, all my answers had been external. It was here with God that I finally embraced a new dream, and the journey for me truly began. I was unable to find my destiny until I got alone with God. It wasn't love or affection that drove me to women. It was the fear of myself. It was as if God were saying, "Scott, have you forgotten who you are?" And I had.

All of us have something we use to medicate our loneliness. For me it was women and relationships, but it could be alcohol, food, drugs, depression, working out, or anything that drives you deeper into that hole. Until you are willing to go into the dark night of the soul and face these fears, you will remain lost. It's time to examine your life and reevaluate where you belong and what you are hiding in a life of addiction. The only one you can really hold onto in this world is God—not women, not food, not alcohol, not drugs, not relationships, not work, not eating disorders, or any other person or thing. When you finally let go of those things, God will fill that void with Himself, and He will be enough.

There is a gift that awaits all of us who confront our fears: we begin to grow. After Jesus came out of the desert where He was tempted for forty days by the devil, He was able to go into the ministry of sharing with others the experience of God. He wants us to find this same gift, the gift of knowing who we are and who we can be in Christ. Paul, Peter, and David were all ordinary men with flaws, yet they were transformed by the grace of God and His gift of redemption.

There are two incredible examples in the Bible of God excavating dead dreams and awakening hearts. In Ezekiel 37, we can read the story of the valley of dry bones. The dry bones are like buried dreams—dreams that have been so forgotten that it seems impossible to ever awaken them again. But God can make these dry bones live! He can resurrect dead dreams and make them come to life. In the story, we see how He breathed life into the most lifeless dream and awakened a heart that had been void, not unlike a life that has been addicted and buried in dependencies. He brought dry, dead bones back to life.

The other example is the story of Jesus's friend Lazarus, who had been dead for many days (John 11). When Jesus came to the tomb, the people warned Him of the putrid smell. You see, Jesus had arrived late—many days after the burial. But instead of entering the smelly grave,

Jesus stood at the tomb and commanded Lazarus to come out. Lazarus walked out as if nothing had happened, as if he'd been napping. I don't know about you, but when I read these stories I hear that same voice telling my dry life to live again! When I passed through the dark night of the soul with God, I saw my dry heart, remembered what I had lost, and the grief was unbearable.

Fear had buried my dreams deep within my heart. Like the valley of dry bones, it was beyond my power to resurrect them. But God could. He put me on the path of my destiny. Have you forgotten who you are? The way you answer will reveal the condition of your heart.

## REFLECTION QUESTIONS

Have you experienced "a dark night of the soul"? Describe what the experience was like.

We began talking about powerlessness in this chapter. Because of our fears, we constantly try to control every aspect of our lives. What fears in your life do you need to relinquish control over?

In what ways have you been controlling you life, depending on your own resources apart from God?

Do you feel that God is beginning to awaken a forgotten or new dream in your heart? What might that dream be?

## REFLECTIONS

## REFLECTIONS

## CHAPTER FOUR

# COURAGE: THE HEART OF FAITH

*Be on your guard; stand firm in the faith;*
*be men of courage; be strong.*

1 CORINTHIANS 16:13 NIV

## LIVING YOUR DASH

If we look at the human condition on a superficial level, we might see a tragic existence. Here is the truth: we are born, we live for a brief period, and then we die. The grave is inevitable for all of us. It's what we do with that brief period of time between birth and death that matters. On most tombstones, there is a birth year, a death year, and a dash that separates the two. "Living your dash" is just another way of saying, "Make the most of your time here on earth." In the middle of the sprint of living that dash, there will no doubt be unlimited difficulties. Life is sometimes unfair and can leave us in an undesirable place. You can't always avoid these situations or control them. But you do have a choice to make: you can either manage your life by an illusion of control, or you can embrace the human condition and live with courage.

## COURAGE TO SURRENDER

All throughout Jesus's ministry, He told people that the way to freedom and abundant life was to surrender. Jesus's own life is the ultimate example of this truth. He gave His life completely, to the point of death. I do not believe there was ever a more free heart than His. And at the same time, I do not believe there was a more courageous person than Christ. He gave it all. The courage to pour out our lives completely for others comes from Him. It's the true response of faith.

I lived the first half of my life in complete self-service. Everything was all about me. And as I have said before, there is not a more selfish person on the planet than an addict. Even when addicts appear to be giving, their motives are what they can get in return. Addicts are motivated to control the world for their own desires, using whomever or whatever to fill emptiness. Is it any wonder that addicts are always thirsty and can never get enough to quench their thirst?

When I got into recovery, the amazing transformation in my life was that God asked me to give it up to him. One of the twelve steps asks the individual to surrender his life 100 percent to God. God does not just ask for my addiction, He asks for everything, especially my heart. I do not think I am alone when I say surrendering is not easy. It's human nature to resist giving up control. When I went through my transformation, I began to die to self. And the most amazing thing happened: I was able to be available to others. I found my life. I found what Christ said in the Bible to be true: "Those who try to hold on to their lives will give up true life. Those who give up their lives for me will hold on to true life" (Matt. 10:39 NCV).

Everyone in the Bible who began their service for God with ulterior motives ended up broken upon their own deceptions. Jonah began his ministry with the hidden intention of seeing the Ninevites destroyed, or at least punished in some way. But when God had compassion on the Ninevites, it sent Jonah into a tailspin. He admitted his displeasure with God: "I knew that you are a God who is kind and shows mercy. You don't become angry quickly, and you have great love. I knew you would choose not to cause harm. So now I ask you, LORD, please kill me. It is better for me to die than to live" (Jonah 4:2–3 NCV). How's that for overreacting? But we do the same thing. We whine and are devastated when our selfish goals fail.

It takes courage for us to relinquish our own desires for God's. Courage is Shadrach, Meshach, and Abednego refusing to renounce God when threatened with the fiery furnace. They would not bow down to an earthly king. They had faith in the One who could deliver them from such a grave situation, but they also had the courage to face death if God chose not to deliver them in the way they hoped. They believed God would take care of them one way or the other—in life or in death. This kind of courage is at the heart of faith.

## FAITH AS COURAGE

When Debbie came to Restore Ministries, she was struggling in a difficult relationship. She came to realize the issues that needed to be addressed and set to work on them—even if meant the relationship had to end. Debbie had the courage to move on from that destructive relationship and began to flourish. But soon after she ended things, she found out that she was pregnant. She was terrified, and her first response was to have an abortion. But with the support of her small group at Restore and a lot of talking with God, Debbie decided to have the baby. It was a bold move, especially because her parents struggled with her decision. But by facing her fears and moving forward with courage, she improved her relationship with her parents, and now she has a beautiful child.

## Craig's Story

Craig's courage began to develop only when he had been forced to turn control over. He'd been stripped of power, and emptied, and he had nothing left but to turn himself—an empty vessel—over to God for filling. It was courage that God began to pour into him. As Craig's faith grew, and he became more dependent on God, courage was the natural result.

"Courage is really a challenge—it's something you have to work on daily because your addictions are always going to be in your body. They're like germs that are just waiting for us to go out in the cold without a sweater on, to be activated and to make us sick. So I have an awareness that I'm living with those addictions and those fears, but I'm going to use courage to keep them at bay, so that they don't overtake my life again."

Craig is adamant in saying that the source of his courage is not in him. He has no way to combat his own fears, he says, except to accept the fact that God has the power to throw whatever He wants to at him. And that this is okay.

"I've accepted Jesus as my friend, who I can talk to any time of day that I want. And I do that—or I'll journal and write down my thoughts, or even listen to Christian music. I find that I have to do things during the day that keep me focused on Jesus, so that I can't lose sight of where I want to go."

Jesus gives us a great example of what it means to live out faith through courage. Anxiety plagued Jesus in the Garden of Gethsemane. The Scriptures say He sweat drops of blood. Then Jesus made one of the most courageous statements of faith. He said, "My Father, if it is not possible for this cup to be taken away unless I drink it, may your will be done" (Matt. 26:42 NIV). Jesus made a decision to live out His faith and go to the cross. He did the heroic act.

We all face moments of decision when we have to be courageous. Troubled times demand that we be heroic. Maybe you're going through turmoil or trouble. Perhaps you are bearing a burden for someone else.

Now is the time to act heroic and be courageous. Remember, courage is in the heart. There is no dress rehearsal in life, and we only get the dash—one shot at living a courageous life. So don't quit. Live your dash.

## THE COURAGE TO SACRIFICE

At Restore Ministries we work with people who suffer from addictions that they are afraid to give up. But why are they so afraid? Perhaps they fear nothing can replace these addictive urges. Some fear that the empty void will be worse than the addiction. But God promises to never leave or forsake us.[1] That means that if He asks us to lay our addictions, our substances, our false idols down at the altar, then He will fill the void. He has promised to always provide us with a way out. "The only temptation that has come to you is that which everyone has. But you can trust God, who will not permit you to be tempted more than you can stand. But when you are tempted, he will also give you a way to escape so that you will be able to stand it" (1 Cor. 10:13 NCV). The thing to notice is how Paul states that every temptation is common among the human race, which means we aren't alone when tempted. But we may feel alone, as if we are the only ones who have a specific temptation. Yet it's not true. We all experience temptation, and we all have a way out.

And that's the key: looking for the way out. Seek the solution that resolves your temptation by exchanging it with one of the fruits of the Spirit: "But the Spirit produces the fruit of love, joy, peace, patience, kindness, goodness, faithfulness, gentleness, self-control" (Gal. 5:22–23 NCV). Each time you are tempted, look for one of the fruits that seems to be the opposite of your temptation. If you're tempted to hate someone, then make a conscious effort to love that person instead. If you're tempted to worry, then exchange it for peace. God's way out is a sacrifice of courage. We need to follow that example. When we sacrifice sin for a season, we can reap everlasting joy. God will fill the void with the fruits of His Spirit.

Many times we are dependent upon ourselves, our intellect, or on others to help free us. Eventually these things take the place of God, and we depend on them more than we depend on Him. There are many undependable things in life, and eventually we understand that the only true and lasting thing is God's love for us. "Yes, I have loved you with an everlasting love; Therefore with lovingkindness I have drawn you" (Jer. 31:3 NKJV).

Let me make an important point about courage: it will never be the absence of fear. Rather, courage means simply showing up and walking through the fear. It's doing the right thing in the face of fear—running through it instead of running from it. The sooner we face our fear and deal with it, the better off we will be. So don't delay. Take on your fears, and exchange them with a fruit of the Spirit.

## FACING OUR FAILURES WITH COURAGE

One of my favorite movies of all time is *Seabiscuit*. It has all the elements of a great drama: it is based on a true story and the main characters face great trials with courage to overcome failures. When self-made millionaire Charles Howard's son dies an accidental death, his wife leaves him, and depression sinks in. Wandering aimlessly, he meets another worn-out soul, horse trainer Tom Smith. Together, they find a difficult horse with potential, Seabiscuit, and begin to work with him. Enter Red Pollard, a down-on-his-luck jockey with a knack for working with difficult horses. All the characters in the story are facing their own fears: the fear of living, the fear of being hurt, the fear of being alone. But with great courage, they all face their challenges and past failures and develop faith in each other and in their own destinies. By the end of the movie, there is victory and redemption. The characters help "fix" each other.

In the final scenes of the movie, Red finishes a difficult race and triumphantly raises his arm in victory. In the faces of the other characters is victory as well, because they all feel as if they have been a part of something larger than life. They feel the redemption that their tremendous journey of courage has produced. And that gives them each an incredible sense of satisfaction. They overcame their fears and defeated the odds.

Courage has different elements. To be courageous, we must act on our own behalf. We have to show up and do the work. We must have the faith to meet each challenge and the vulnerability to ask for help and depend on others. And, ultimately, we must let God orchestrate our lives behind the scenes.

## REFLECTION QUESTIONS

What do you think of when you hear the word *surrender*? Does it have a positive or negative connotation to you?

What is one thing you can do to help you focus on God—to help you find courage in difficult times?

Share a moment or incident you've faced that required courage.

What specific temptation are you facing right now? Which fruit of the Spirit might counteract that temptation (see Galatians 5:22–23)?

Can you have courage if there is no fear? What is a situation in your life that you need to face with courage?

## REFLECTIONS

## REFLECTIONS

## REFLECTIONS

## CHAPTER FIVE

# LIVING A FULFILLED LIFE

*"At least I galloped! When did you?"*

—MARTIN DYSART IN *EQUUS*

## MOTIVATION AND INSPIRATION

In the Southeastern Conference of college football, there has always been a great rivalry between University of Alabama and Auburn University. In one memorable game, back in the days when Bear Bryant was coaching Alabama and Pat Dye was the coach for Auburn team, Alabama's first-string quarterback was injured, so they were left with the second-string quarterback. On opposing team's twenty-yard line, ahead by five points, and with two minutes left in the game, it was first down for Alabama. Bear Bryant yelled into the helmet of the second-string quarterback, "Whatever you do, do not pass! Run the ball all four plays. And then if we have to hold them, our defense will get us through and we will win."

The quarterback ran onto the field full of zeal and determination. First down, they gained no yardage. Second down, Auburn held 'em. Third down, they gained a yard. Fourth down came and the hand-off was somehow muffled, leaving the quarterback with the ball. Running around the backfield, he looked in the end zone and saw the split end ready to catch the ball. So he passed it. What he failed to see was the fastest man on the field, the safety for the Auburn team, who also saw the pass coming. The Auburn safety maneuvered himself in front of the receiver, intercepted the ball, and started racing down the field. The quarterback, normally not very fast himself, raced down the field, caught the safety and tackled him, securing the win for Alabama.

Coach Dye later said to Bear Bryant, "I read the scouting reports, and that second-string quarterback is supposed to be slow. How is it he caught up with the fastest man on the field?"

Bryant replied, "It's very simple. Your man was running for the goal line and a touchdown. My man was running for his life!"[1]

On this journey to freedom you will need powerful motivation, because in many ways you are running for your life. Maintaining inspiration and motivation will be the key to successfully overcoming fear. Fear is the ultimate demotivator. It makes us retreat from our goals, urging us to give up, to quit, to stop trying. Fear tells us that the situation is hopeless, that it's useless to try. Motivation keeps us moving forward, no matter what the cost and no matter how painful the process is. We often miss great rewards in life because we give up too soon, instead of persevering and striving to maintain motivation.

Motivation, perseverance, and inspiration are three cords of one rope. All three are fueled by vision or a purpose that inspires us. Inspiration stirs our passions, and out of this inspiration a motivation arises. We are motivated to persevere by the thing that inspires us. Great coaches like Vince Lombardi, Knute Rockne, and Bear Bryant had the ability to inspire their players and help them reach their full potential. They encouraged players to fight through the pain and overcome obstacles to achieve success.

We all want to achieve something. But many of us won't persevere without proper motivation. When motivation wanes, so does the desire to keep going. When we're properly motivated, we're willing to work hard, to sacrifice, and to do whatever it takes to achieve success. Inspiration produces the change we want in life.

Inspiration can come from almost anywhere. The key is to maintain our motivation and work toward accomplishing a goal. Inspiration comes from outside ourselves—from seeing, feeling, or hearing something that compels us to respond. Motivation, on the other hand, needs to be internal. It's what drives us to work toward our goal. It makes us get up in the morning and go to the gym, rather than sleep in. It pushes us to take those extra classes or study when we could be watching TV. Motivation is the action stemming from the inspiration. The lifeblood of any goal is motivation. We must maintain the motivation in order to achieve the goal.

You've heard that fear is a powerful motivator. And it is true that some people are motivated by nagging thoughts such as, *If I don't do this I will get in trouble.* Take Bear Bryant's quarterback, for example. The coach said he was running for his life. Yes, he ran after the safety out of fear. But that type of motivation never lasts, because fear-based motivation is external. Motivation must be intrinsic in order to push us past the wavering emotions of today.

In his book *Personal Best*, Dr. George Sheehan writes, "Action is always impelled by some good we want to obtain." He goes on to explain that if we lose this motivation to be mission driven, to strive for our best then, "We will settle for less than our best, and diminish our lives and our possibilities."[2] You see, when we are inspired and motivated, we are pushing forward toward the mission that only we can fulfill. As we fulfill our purpose, fear will jump right in the middle of our motivation and try to paralyze us. Fear will tell us to quit because we might be hurt, crushed, or, even worse, that we will fail. Fear says, "You can't do this. Get off. Back away."

Too often, we sell ourselves short and our lives as well. When our horizons narrow, our goals do too. We settle for a comfortable passing grade. We groove through life, effortlessly passing our days. But the intensity of our art—our lives—and therefore our joy, passes as well. But that is part of the bargain. Dr. Sheehan encourages us with, "My end is not simple happiness. My need, drive and desire is to achieve my full and complete self. If I do what I have come to do, if I create that life I was made for, then happiness will follow. The problem in motivation is not the dedication and effort and sacrifice needed to get what I want, it is knowing what it is we could and must begin with."[3]

We will have setbacks, things will throw us off course, and some of us will quit too soon. That's why I believe that God is such an intricate part of change in our lives—because He is the ultimate inspiration. Dr. Sheehan reminds us, "No motivation can live where faith and courage are absent."[4] True motivation comes from an inspired vision coupled with enthusiasm. Courage will grow in us, because it is tied to our faith. God can inspire us, and give us a vision of what He wants us to become or what he wants us to accomplish in life. But then it comes down to us having courage to keep going in the face of pain. The book of James tells us to count it all joy, because trials in our lives help us grow and develop character (James 1:2–12). God wants us to be the best we can be, and He knows that great motivation requires faith and courage. We see this in action at Restore Ministries. When faith and courage are present, we see the greatest change in people's lives. They begin to live the lives they were meant to live.

## Craig's Story

In the worst of times, Craig began to discover the faith-based life.

"I forced myself to go to church one day and saw the sign-up information about Restore Ministries, and so I signed up for Journey to Freedom out of total desperation. And JTF became the blueprint that I used to put myself together. This was when I was going through my darkness, when I realized that I was absolutely, totally powerless over all of my fears and relationships and jobs—everything. I began to have a desire to change.

"I came to know that sometimes God allows tremendous pain in our lives, and He makes us realize that there is no one or anything that can help us get out of a bad situation. He allows it so that He can get our attention, to urge us to climb out of those desperate situations and allow Him to heal us. It's not all about just saying 'God heal me'—you have to admit you are powerless, and if you do that, He will help you. I found that, through my depression and loneliness and all kinds of emotions, in one moment I had the realization that there was nothing anything or anyone on this earth could do to help. And that's when I gave it up. And I got on my hands and knees and said, "God, I am powerless. I am willing to let you help me become whole again, and I know the first step in that is change. And I'm ready to change."

This was the beginning of Craig's new life of a healthy kind of dependency. A faith-based life.

God is constantly inspiring me to keep fighting, to keep believing. Even if a task seems beyond my ability, He is there saying, "It is possible. You can beat this addiction and have a new start. Believe in Me—I'm here with you. Together we can overcome this. What may look hopeless to you is not hopeless with Me. Nothing is impossible with Me! Let's fight this good fight."

I can't adequately explain this feeling. It's something you need to experience for yourself. But when we turn our lives back to God and turn completely to Him for motivation, He ignites this fire, this passion, this inspiration in us to change. It motivates us every day to embrace this mission we are on. My primary mission is to continue changing my life for the better every day with God's help. The things I do every day help motivate me to keep going.

Maybe you have a message on your heart that only you can share—perhaps you need to write down your thoughts. Or maybe you need to be a friend to someone else who's hurting. Your mission might be to raise a child in the ways of the Lord. Maybe you're an artist and you need to paint a masterpiece. What's your mission? With God's help, you can discover the mission that only you were meant to complete.

## A LIFE WORTH LIVING

I lost a good friend recently when he was killed in a motorcycle accident. He was only thirty-six years old. Most of us harbor grand illusions about how long we will live. But no matter how careful we are or what precautions we take, something can happen in an instant that is out of our control. But what we do have control over is how we live today. We should not be satisfied with anything less than a life overflowing with vitality. My friend embraced this way of life. He had overcome numerous struggles in his past and continued to strive toward a better life for himself and his wife. He lived with no regrets and tackled anything and everything that came his way. He left behind a legacy that has affected countless lives. Too many of us are walking around like the living dead. We cram ourselves into cars, offices, and department stores—rushing back and forth in a daze. We're missing the picture. My prayer is that you will discover how to live life to the fullest. Never let fear cause you to shrink back. Embrace the inspiration, take the motivation, enjoy the risk, have courage, cling to faith, and see how much grander life tastes.

There is responsibility that comes with freedom, and that can be frightening to some of us. To achieve freedom we are responsible to do whatever it takes to live out a peaceful, satisfied, content life. And though we were created by God to live that way—as free men and women—there is usually a great cost involved. Sometimes we have to give up the things or people in our lives that hold us back or try to control us.

That's why Jesus came to this earth—to set the captives free. We are those captives. Sadly, the vast majority of us like the comfort of being a captive. We are so comfortable in our bondage and misery that we are afraid to truly be free from those chains. Captivity requires no responsibility; it doesn't ask anything of us. When I was captive to my addictions, I became content with the inadequacy of my life. I was comfortable in my depression and cynicism. I didn't expect anything from life or myself, so there was no responsibility, nothing to strive for, and nothing creating a sense of urgency. The man William Wallace, played by Mel Gibson in the movie *Braveheart*, gives a classic speech on the responsibility of freedom. He is prepping his men to enter the greatest battle of their lives. He is giving them the encouragement they need to face their fear of death, the incentive they need to go on. He says that with the possibility of death comes freedom. Freedom for their countrymen, their wives, their children, and generations to come. Wallace asks, "What will you do with that freedom? Will you fight? Will you run? Fight and you might die . . . run and you will live, for a while. They might take our lives but they can never take our freedom!"[5]

Can we live with great courage? Can we face our fears and embrace the valor to fight for our freedom? This is the central idea of Christ. He wants us to live in the absolute zenith of the moment, fully engaged in living the responsibility of freedom in our lives. With that comes purpose, meaning, and a fulfilled life. That is what I am fighting for. What are you fighting for?

Author Marianne Williamson has said, "Our deepest fear is not that we are inadequate. Our deepest fear is that we are powerful beyond measure. It is our light, not our darkness, that frightens us most. We ask ourselves, 'Who am I to be brilliant, gorgeous, talented, and famous?' Actually, who are you not to be? You are a child of God. Your playing small does not serve the world. There is nothing enlightened about shrinking so that people won't feel insecure around you. We were born to make manifest the glory of God that is within us. It's not just in some of us; it's in all of us. And when we let our own light shine, we unconsciously give other people permission to do the same. As we are liberated from our own fear, our presence automatically liberates others."[6]

Who among us wouldn't like to be William Wallace, standing up for what we believe in and living a life free from the fear of tomorrow? That very existence is not far-fetched. You can achieve your own personal freedom if you believe that you can and stand up and fight for it, rather than run from it. Recently, one of the greatest massacres in history occurred

on a college campus here in the United States. I read the story of Liviu
Livrescu, a Professor of Aerospace Engineering at Virginia Tech, who self-
lessly shielded his students from the grotesque massacre that took place
on April 16, 2007. He was a hero that day because he used his body to bar-
ricade the door so that his students could get out the window as the
shooter tried to get into the classroom. A bullet pierced through the door
and killed him.

There were many other heroes on that tragic day, but his story was
extraordinary because of his past. At eight years old he was taken to a
concentration camp during WWII for being of Jewish descent. He sur-
vived the nightmare of the Nazi camp only to be killed on a national
day of remembrance for the Jewish culture of holocaust. Livrescu's
son said in an interview that this heroic act by his father was typical:
"He did not fear death and at all times tried to do the right thing."
Rabbi Marvin Hier, head of the Simon Wiesenthal Center in LA, said
of Livrescu that, "Destiny came knocking on his door. Any survivor of
the Holocaust knows how helpless he felt. This man decided he would
not let this act of evil occur; he was not going to be a bystander."[7]
What an amazing testimony to a life. He did not fear death. He gave
his life for others.

We are all going to die someday. That is a fact. Our time on this earth
is limited, and there is no way we can predict how long it will be. It is
ultimately out of our control. But what we can do is choose not to be a
bystander and watch life slip away. Without courage, we cannot face
the responsibility that our freedom demands. We could not grasp the
potential our days hold; we could not live them to the absolute fullest.
Our legacy and destiny were created to be fulfilled, and without
courage, we can't accomplish it. We need to model ourselves after the
brave men in this chapter. We cannot live in fear any more than we can
live without oxygen. Freedom gives us life. Breathe in the freedom, live
in courage, and fight the good fight! Then, when your time on earth is
up, you'll have left nothing but fierce dignity and a legacy that will be
admired for generations to come.

## PASSION

A therapist friend of mine gave me a copy of Peter Schaffer's play *Equus*. It is a story of a young man who is seeing a psychiatrist because he is declared insane. It seems this deranged fellow took a ride on a horse bareback naked, and then proceeded to gouge the horse's eyes out. Yes, a little demented, but there was a reason for his madness. To him, the horse represented his version of God. He would ride the horse with everything he had—worshiping, believing that the horse was God—and then he would be completely ashamed, knowing that the horse (or God) could see him complete with all his flaws. He was incredibly passionate and utterly insane.

The therapist in the play was a unique man himself. Stagnant in his life, dead in his own world, he has neglected his wife, opting to fill his time with books about travel to exotic places he never visits. He merely exists as a benign person. It makes the reader wonder which character is demented. The kid is trying to worship his god. Most will never feel the passion and dedication he does. And his therapist was barely living. At a pivotal moment, the therapist comes to the realization about this young man and the correlation with his own existence.

He says, "Look, to go through life and call it yours—your life—you first have to get your own pain. Pain that's unique to you. You can't just dip into the common bin and say 'That's enough!'. . . He's done that. All right he's sick. He's full of misery and fear. He was dangerous, and could be again, though I doubt it. But that boy has known a passion more ferocious than I have ever felt in any second of my life. And let me tell you something, I envy it. That is what his stare has been saying to me all this time. 'At least I galloped! When did you?'"[8]

Sometimes I let this statement wash over me. "At least I galloped! Did you?" I wonder if I've lived in merely the ho-hum of existence. Maybe I really haven't galloped, lived with passion, fire, and worship. It is ironic that it takes this crazy boy to reveal the reality of the situation. The kid never intended to portray himself as anything other than what he was.

He worshiped with passion, and Shaffer uses the boy's madness to reveal something to us about our own worship. To miss this is to overlook the whole point of the play. The kid shows how crazy we are when we live dead existences. So my question is: "Have you galloped?"

We can walk through life being fearful of freedom, fearful of loving, and fearful of passion, but where does that get us? Fear tells us to be cautious, to be more efficient with our lives. But Jesus awakens our hearts and dares us to dream, and to dream big. He wants us to believe that there is nothing too big for Him. He wants to bring the adventure back into our human existence. But most of us, instead of facing our fears, shrink back into our shells and only exist. What if William Wallace had feared the enemy? Many villages would've burned, and many deaths would've occurred.

My prayer is that you learn to gallop, to fight, and not be a bystander in your own life. Start taking risks. It's okay to fail, but make sure you get up and ride like the wind! You owe it to yourself.

## REFLECTION QUESTIONS

What do *motivation* and *inspiration* mean to you?

How well do you maintain motivation when fear creeps in? Why do you think this is?

How does maintaining motivation help you persevere through tough times?

In the movie *Braveheart*, William Wallace speaks of the responsibility that comes with freedom. What responsibilities are you afraid of that might come from living a life of freedom?

Do you feel that you have "galloped" in your life? Are you living with passion? Why or why not?

## REFLECTIONS

## REFLECTIONS

## CHAPTER SIX

# THE FAITH-BASED LIFE: THE ANSWER TO FEAR

*"Now faith is being sure of what we hope for and certain of what we do not see."*

HEBREWS 11:1 NIV

Ed came to Restore Ministries to address his sexual addictions. Over the last two years he has experienced incredible growth and healing, especially in his marriage. During his first contact with Restore, his wife viewed a television program about so-called healthy sexual relationships, and it had caused some friction in their marriage. The therapist on the program said spouses should explore their sexual fantasies with each other in the bedroom. After watching this, his wife shared this idea with him. She wondered if it could possibly improve their relationship, so she asked if he had any sexual fantasies. It was the last thing he wanted to discuss with his wife, because fantasies had played a huge role in his addiction. He feared talking about such things with her would put more strain on their marriage. He had no idea how to respond to his wife's exploration. He told her about his sexual addiction and his recovery. He explained his struggle with fantasies and told her they didn't exist anymore. When I asked about his sexual relationship with his wife, he said his desire for sex had waned because he was fearful of a relapse. His sexual relationship with his wife had paid the price because of this fear.

The answer for his recovery wasn't to kill his sexual desire, but to grow it in a healthy sexual relationship driven by intimacy and love with his wife. In this context, their relationship would be reflection of their sincere care for one another, rather than the act of a selfish sexual addiction. This man was allowing his recovery to be driven by fear. We call this being a "dry drunk" or "white knuckling it," as compared to the recovery being driven by growing in faith and being transformed.

Something similar happened to a woman in Restore who has a food addiction. Instead of picking up a drink or a drug to fill the void in her life, she went to food. When she realized her problem, she became fearful of food—any food. The answer for her recovery was not for her to become anorexic and starve herself, but to learn how to control her eating habits. If she is being driven by the fear of eating, she is still being controlled by food—just at the opposite end of the spectrum. She had a food phobia that had started as an attraction addiction but had morphed into an aversion addiction.

*Attraction addictions* are to something pleasurable that a person uses to fill the hole in their soul. Their addiction is to the pleasure of escape. But an *aversion addiction* is the fear of the addiction. We will use whatever means available to avoid the pleasure. You can't overcome either type of addiction until the fear is removed.

## Craig's Story

Craig's new motivation has sprung from a new relationship: "What I tried to do before was to be a church Christian. I would go to church only when I wanted something or I needed help from God. It's like I invited Jesus to Stony River Steaks on Saturday nights for dinner, and we'd talk over steak and a bottle of wine, and then I'd say, "See you

·later." Then I'd look in the rearview mirror, and He'd be standing there in the door with a puzzled look on His face. But I realized that what it's all about is inviting Him over—to live in my house and never leave.

"My motivation to move forward in life is the knowledge that I never want to go through that darkness again. My years of fear and codependency were the lowest point of my life. Now, being in my forties, it's all about finishing life strong and being fulfilled, with faith and happiness. So that alone motivates me on a daily basis. I try to live every day asking what I can do to please God, because He's doing things that I don't even know about, and He will provide grace and everything else that I need to live. For that reason, I'm no longer codependent on a relationship with anybody else because I have one with Him. And I feel like there is somebody out there that He wants me to be with, but I'm not going to push for it. That attitude makes it easier to live my life every day, fully."

Craig no longer lives a life controlled by fear of decisions or of loneliness. He has discovered the passionate lifestyle that comes with being able to make choices—with the freedom that dependence on God can provide.

The hope of recovery is that God transforms us from the inside out, making us new men and women. Looking at both stories above, these two were both trying to control their recovery, rather than allowing God to transform them. If fear is controlling our addiction, then we are still not in a place of recovery. We have not recovered if we are using the "dry drunk" or "white knuckling" methods—we're simply ignoring the issue. To truly be recovered from an addiction, any addiction, we have to be transformed.

Mike's recovery can begin the moment he turns his lust to genuine love. The woman's recovery from food addiction will begin when she stops consoling herself with food and develops a healthy relationship with food. Both of these life-controlling issues stem from fear. Two of the greatest pleasures God gave us in life are food and sex. Both, in the proper context, bring us pleasure. Yet addicts allow these blessings from God to become methods of control and fear in their lives. This demonstrates how anything can become an addiction when an individual is driven by fear.

The healing aspect of recovery is our faith. When we come to the end of our ropes and let go of the fear of these addictions, we're taking a leap of faith. We overcome our fear by trusting God will be there to help us. Anytime we trust ourselves to be strong enough to do things on our own, we ultimately fail. But, if we live by faith, putting our trust in the Lord, we will flourish. We will be free to live amazing lives.

I encourage everyone to go through the twelve steps with Christ and work through this process of transformation. In my ten years of working with people through the twelve steps, I have seen it free people from every possible life-controlling issue.[1]

## BRINGING THE PAST INTO THE LIGHT

Many people are afraid of revealing their pasts. They are afraid something they've done or something done to them will negatively affect the present. This was a huge issue for me in my journey to freedom. I was so afraid of people discovering things I'd done that it sabotaged my recovery as well as my ability to have quality, intimate relationships. Certainly the past will affect the future. That's why it's so important to bring things to the light. Burying old wounds keeps us in bondage to them, isolated in fear. As long as we keep secrets, we are being controlled by the fear of our past, and that prevents us from fully embracing the present.

My past is not a secret anymore. My past is a wonderful gift that can help other people overcome their addictions and give them hope. It has no power over my life anymore—it's just my story, one of healing, redemption, and recovery. Every time I get to share my story, it has the possibility of bringing hope to those who might be in the same struggles. None of this would be happening if I hadn't brought my past into the light and walked in it every day by God's grace and for His glory. It all comes from living a faith-based life versus living in fear of my past.

## THE REALITY OF RELAPSE

Relapse is always a possibility in recovery. When it happens, we have two options: 1) we can helplessly stay in a state of relapse, or 2) we can get back into our recovery programs and learn from our relapse. To truly learn and heal from it, we need to confess our setback to God and others. Remember, relapse is not permanent. It is only a temporary setback.

## LEARNING THE TRIGGERS

The outside forces that lead us into relapse are called *triggers*. Triggers help create a temptation in us. A food addict may face temptation when they walk past the pastry display at a grocery store, or see a certain commercial for their favorite fast-food joint. An anxious feeling could come over them, causing them to want to medicate with food. For an alcoholic, temptation may come at a restaurant or a sporting event where they used to drink. These places or moments trigger the desire for their old drug of choice. An individual can be in recovery for years, even successfully, and certain things will still trigger the memory or the desire for a "fix." And even as an addict gives in to this trigger, the inner critic continues to chip away at his self-worth, *I always knew you were a failure. Now this proves it. You'll never change so why try? Give up.* But in recovery, we refuse to listen to negative self-talk. We replace it with a positive message: *You possess an incredible testimony that someone needs to hear. You can overcome your fears and help so many people.* That's the voice I choose to listen to.

The same thing works in our response to fear. Certain situations are going to trigger old fears. A long-held fear may be present for the rest of your life. But how you respond to these fears will make all the difference. Defeat them by acknowledging they're there, and then focus your attention on a new and courageous response. Don't allow fear to deter you from your path. When old fears rear their ugly heads, ask God to give you strength to have a new response to fear. Over time, those fears will diminish in strength, and your new life will become strong.

A faith-based life grows out of a relationship with God. I'm not talking about structured religiosity or a set of rules and religious dogma, but rather an authentic relationship with God. You start by talking to God every day. Work through the twelve steps, and trust God to guide you. His grace is always working in and through us. Before I believed in God, I assumed I had control over my life. In reality, my life was completely out of control. I remained trapped in my addiction—self-destructing and dying on the inside. Living by faith and making God the controller of my existence eliminated my fear. I no longer felt alone.

For an alcoholic, giving up one drink at a time is living a faith-based life. Living a faith-based life means we accept God's grace and love for us. He tells us that perfect love casts out all fear. The grace He wants us to experience is perfect love. This is why a faith-based life is the answer to overcoming our deepest fears. I have lived both ways—in faith and in fear—and I will never want to go back to a fear-based life. A fear-based life leads to bondage. We weren't meant to be slaves, bogged down by life. We were meant to live faith-based lives of freedom! God, in His infinite wisdom, knew how afraid we were and would be. He knew that we needed a Savior, a Shepherd who would care for His flock. That's why He sent Jesus.

You can't *learn* freedom in a church service or a Bible study. You have to *experience* it when you are being authentic and honest with God. It helps to be surrounded by people who are on that same path of recovery, people who will share your journey. These are the same people who will ultimately hold you accountable to stay on the path. In this environment, your life can be transformed. You'll see a hint of fulfillment—

that this life can evolve into everything you ever dreamed of. That, my friends, only comes from living a life of faith.

A faith-based life takes courage. You'll have to confront your fears, stare them down, and truly become free. I pray this will be your experience. Seize the future and embrace tomorrow!

## REFLECTION QUESTIONS

Describe what a fear-based life looks like.

Describe what a faith-based life looks like.

How has fear controlled your life?

What do you think God is telling you when he says, "perfect love casts out all fear"?

What steps can you begin taking today to build a faith-based life?

What do you think your life would be like if you lived by faith? Be as specific as possible.

## REFLECTIONS

# MY PERSONAL PLAN OF CHANGE

## SAMPLE PLAN OF CHANGE

Read through the following sample Personal Plan of Change before completing your own plan.

> *Self-Assessment:* My name is Kim and I am thirty-two years old. I suffer from serious anxiety and panic attacks that seem to occur more often than not. Anything can trigger them, but it seems they become rampant when I begin thinking about my future. My career and love life has been steadily on the decline for the last decade, and I am afraid that I won't ever have the family I am dreaming of. I try to find solace in men, and relationships in general, but I got so burned in the last one that I'm not sure that I need a relationship anymore. I have succumbed to the idea that my life is what it is, and I don't think that I can or want to try to change it. I am afraid that I am going to die alone and that I am not strong enough to ever be different. I am afraid that God won't ever accept anyone like me—so why change now?

### Step One

> *Spirit:* I fear that I have no purpose in life and that I am not living up to my true potential. So because of that I am not really striving to do well in my job, and I have quit going to church.

*Mind:* I fear that the change itself won't be as good as what I hope it will be. I would rather stay here in my little existence and not attempt it, because every time I try to change it never works.

*Body:* I fear that whenever I get a man in my life and he figures out all the terrible things that I have done, he will break up with me and then I will be alone again and heartbroken. I would rather never know that feeling again, so I try to stay away from men in general.

## Step Two

*Spirit:* I want to learn how to be active in my own life and strive to live a life that has importance and meaning. I will work at giving my best in my job, and I will start going to church again. I will take time to reflect and think weekly about how my fears have been driving me inward into a place of isolation.

*Mind:* I want to get over the fear of changing. The fact is that I will have to change in order to get the results I am looking for. I will make strides to get out of my comfort zone, and I will journal to get past the old thoughts that I have, replacing them with a new positive outlook.

*Body:* I want to find a meaningful, satisfying relationship where I can be vulnerable and open to the possibility of a future with someone, regardless of the past. I will begin by staying true to myself. I will begin dating occasionally. I will be honest and upfront about my past as the conversation comes up. I will be okay if someone rejects me, because I know that someday I will find the one who complements me.

## Step Three

Support Community:
    women's small group at church
    twelve-step program
Individual Support:
    Beth (church mentor)
    Jessie (long time friend and supporter)
    pastor at church
    Susan (accountability partner)

## Step Four

My life will evolve into something that I never thought it would be—peaceful. I won't have to worry so much about my very existence on this earth and what I am here for. I can wake up every day and strive to be the best that I can be—to live my life the way I have always dreamed. I can have good relationships that will build me up and encourage me to push for the change in my life. I will be transformed into a new person. There won't be any more panic or anxiety attacks. Instead there will be laughter and happiness.

## Step Five

Lord, I know that I have put my trust in myself for too long. I know now that I can't do this thing, this life, without You to pull me through. I am not strong enough, and I don't have the capability to control anything. I don't want to fear the unknown anymore, or wonder where I belong. I am ready to be powerless over myself and my fears. I am ready for You to take them from me and transform me from the inside out. I trust You for a husband that will accept me for who I am and as the creation that You made me to be. I give my future to You; I give these fears to You. Amen.

# CREATING YOUR PERSONAL PLAN OF CHANGE

## Step One

Create a daily plan of action that will help you achieve a faith-based life versus a fear-based life. Under each of the following headings, write down the fears that relate to that particular part of your life. Find a couple of close friends or sponsors you can trust and share your fears with them. Allow these people to be your support group and help you through this transformation of releasing your fears to God.

*Spirit* (for example: fear of dying alone, meaninglessness, fulfilled life, etc.)

*Mind* (for example: fear of anxiety, not being good enough, the responsibility of freedom, etc.)

*Body* (for example: fear of not physically being able to give up something, what will replace the hole, etc.)

## Step Two

Establish motivation and inspiration. Write individual goals for each fear and create specific steps that will move you toward a life of freedom in your spirit, mind, and body.

*Spirit*

*Mind*

*Body*

## Step Three

Find a support team. Here are some suggested resources:

A local support community
Restore Ministries (www.restoreymca.org)
Alcoholics Anonymous (www.alcoholics-anonymous.org)
Overeaters Anonymous (www.oa.org)
Sexaholics Anonymous (www.saa-recovery.org)
Al Anon (www.al-anon.org)
Narcotics Anonymous (www.na.org)

List at least one individual in each category below who will support you and share your journey to recovery.

Friend:
Sponsor:
Therapist:
Counselor:
Doctor:
Pastor:
Life Coach:
Personal Trainer:
Nutritionist:
Physical Therapist:
Other:

## Step Four

Write a brief description of your faith-based life and how it differs from the fear-based life you conquered. Include a mission statement that encompasses the way you will live as a person free from fear.

## Step Five

Write a prayer that you can recite every day as you are working through this liberation from your fears.

How we deal with the fear in our lives is one of the most important challenges we will face as human beings. Our responses to fear truly determine everything—our responses will either shape our lives in a positive, constructive manner or they will lead us down a destructive path, preventing us from living our lives to the fullest. If we do not learn to live a life of courage we will end up shrinking back and hiding from life.

God tells us over and over to be of great courage and not to live in fear. For our hearts can only be free when we realize that freedom is found in faith. In Psalms 23: 4 says that, "Even if I walk through a very dark valley, I will not be afraid, because you are with me" (NCV). And in Isaiah 41:10, God says "So do not fear, for I am with you; do not be dismayed, for I am your God. I will strengthen you and help you; I will uphold you with my righteous right hand" (NIV).

We can overcome our fears when we learn to live a life grounded in faith to a God that promises never to leave us.

# TIPS FOR LEADING A JOURNEY TO FREEDOM SMALL GROUP

Welcome and thank you for accepting the challenge of leading others along their own journeys to freedom. These tips are designed to aid you in creating a small group setting that is productive and full of hope, health, and happiness.

## PREPARATION

Being well prepared will help alleviate any anxiety you may have about leading your group. When you know what you want to accomplish in your group, it will help you stay on track with the lesson plan. Plus, if you're not prepared, participants will pick up on your lack of preparation, which might affect their own dedication to the group and the process of change. In extreme cases, lack of preparation may even cause you to lose some participants. If the leader is not committed, why should the participants be committed? So come to your group prepared to lead them.

Be a role model. A good facilitator is simply a model group participant. Be on time. Be prepared. Do your homework. Guard against moodiness.

Be consistent. Be positive. Be a good listener. Maintain confidentiality. Be enthusiastic.

Recognize your limitations. It is important that you remember that you are not responsible for the results of your group. You are not responsible to "fix" anyone. You are not a counselor, a therapist, or a minister. You are a mentor, one who is helping guide another down a path that you have traveled before. Each participant is responsible for his or her own life and journey.

## OPENING THE GROUP SESSION

Use gentleness and patience as you pace the progress of the group. Rushing through the lessons might be exhausting for your participants. Try to find some kind of meaningful devotional, excerpt from a book, or song to emphasize and complement what you are studying for the week.

Plan your time so that you are able to get through the majority of the recommended questions in each less on, but more important, be prepared to settle for quality of questions and answers over quantity. The goal is to have a productive meeting. Getting through every question in the lesson may seem optimal, but it may not accomplish the goal.

## BE AWARE

Avoid being the center of attention during group time. Your role as leader is to get the group involved in sharing, to keep the discussion moving forward and on topic, and to make sure that your group is on time and the necessary material is covered. You are there to give direction and guidance to the group, but avoid dominating the group by talking too much in the sessions.

Be aware of your group dynamics. As a facilitator, get to know your group members. In order to help them as much as possible, you need to be aware and in tune with their needs. Pay attention to the members' body language, their actions, and what they are saying and sharing. Assess the participants in their response and in their openness (or lack of).

Don't let any one member dominate the group. Handling the "talker" in your group will require some skill. Be careful, because if one member begins to dominate your group, it can alienate some of the more reserved members. If one member is opening up and sharing for long periods of time, try not to let this member's problems control the group. Say, "I would love to continue this discussion with you after the meeting. Will that be okay?" This will keep you from appearing uncaring and will give the group permission to get back on track. Also, think about positioning. Sit beside these individuals instead of across from them to avoid prolonged eye contact. When presenting a question or topic for discussion, put a time limit on responses. If someone runs over the limit, don't be afraid to break in and praise the person's point, but then raise a new question back to the group about what was shared. Validate the individual's feelings and input, but then focus the discussion.

Allow silence. Often, facilitators become uncomfortable with silence in group discussions. Sometimes it is good to have a moment of silence so that the participants will speak up and start owning the conversation. Do not feel like you have to fill the void. If the group members think you are going to fill the silence, then they will learn to wait for you. If you find that there has been a considerable amount of time given to answer a question and no one is speaking up, you might ask them why they are silent or move on to another question.

Contain the desire to rescue. If someone gets emotionally upset or begins to cry and show emotion during the session, avoid anything that could interfere with the member feeling the emotion of the moment. Let the individual express the emotions and deal with them, even if they are painful. While the person is sharing, do not reach over and hug, touch, or comfort. After the individual has finished sharing and is done, then offer a hug if you desire or thank and affirm the person for speaking courageously.

Use self-disclosure appropriately. One element of being a good facilitator is a willingness to be vulnerable and to share your journey of change at the appropriate times. However, be careful that you do not use the group to deal with your unresolved issues.

As you lead discussion, consistently state and reiterate the boundaries of group discussion—confidentiality about what is spoken in the group, respect for each other, and the right to pass if a member doesn't feel comfortable sharing at the time. Accept what each person has to say without making sudden judgments. Be the primary catalyst in providing a warm, open, trusting, and caring atmosphere. This will help the group gradually take ownership.

## CLOSING THE GROUP

Manage your time wisely. It is important that your group start and end on time. Strive for consistency, beginning with the first meeting by starting and ending on time and continuing that schedule each week.

## SESSION ONE—INTRODUCTION WEEK

### Lesson Goal:

In your first meeting you will not cover any material. You will begin to get to know each other as a group and learn the structure and guidelines for the next eight weeks, as well as the expectations of each participant.

### Leading the Session:

Welcome the participants and commend them on taking this action to pursue change in their lives.

Ask each participant to share whatever information they are

comfortable sharing about themselves with the group: name, occupa-tion, number and ages of children and or grandchildren, where you were born, how you heard of this group, etc. are good places to start. Be sure that you and your co-facilitator (if applicable) introduce yourselves first to increase the group's comfort level.

Show the first session of Scott Reall's video (if applicable), talk about what they have to look forward to as a group in the upcoming eight weeks, and present group guidelines to the participants:

Confidentiality is of the utmost importance.
Group members are not required to talk but encouraged to do so.
Agree to accept each other and to encourage one another.
We do not give advice, or try to "fix" or rescue other group members.
Be honest.
Be on time.
Agree to make the weekly meetings and the daily work a priority.

Ask if anyone would like to ask a question or add a group guideline. The goal is for participants to feel safe, secure and encouraged.

Choose one of the following warm-up questions to open up the group and begin to break the ice:

What do you like to do when you have free time?
What brings you great joy?
What is a special talent or skill that you possess?

Pair your group into couples, and give each person five minutes to answer the following questions to each other:

What brought you here today?
What in your life do you want to change?
What excuses will you give yourself to not come to group or do your homework?

## Closing the Group

Encourage the group members to come back to the next meeting.

Encourage group members to read and answer the questions at the end of the chapter to be discussed next week and to write their answers in the blank space provided. Tell them to come next week ready to discuss.

Assign accountability partners for each participant and, if possible, pair them with the partner that they were paired with for the last exercise. Ask them to exchange phone numbers and e-mail addresses.

Accountability Partner Guidelines:

Discuss the specifics of the change each person is trying to achieve.

Relate how each person is doing in spirit, mind, and body.

Ask your partner about his or her struggles, problems, and particular difficulties.

Be considerate of each other's time and situations, and remember that the purpose is to discuss change.

Make an effort to take the conversation beyond a superficial level.

The Importance of Accountability Partners:

One of the best tools to help us through the rough times in our journey to freedom is accountability. Often we don't realize how much accountability has influenced and affected our decisions throughout our lives. We are accountable to get to work on time or we may lose our jobs. In school, athletes have to keep their grades up, attend class, and get to practice or they are off the team. In the same way, unless we have some sort of accountability, many of us will not sustain our efforts to change. We need accountability to develop the discipline of sticking with something, especially if consistency is hard for us.

Be sure and thank them for coming this week. Express how excited you are to be with them and to discover where this journey is going to take all of you as a group.

Close with prayer, singing, saying the serenity prayer, or any positive way you feel appropriate.

## SESSIONS 2 THROUGH 7—COVERING THE STUDY GUIDE MATERIAL

For these six weeks, you will be covering Chapters 1 through 6 in the study guide. You will want to follow and review the guidelines for preparing for leading a small group. Once each session begins thank everyone for being there and then begin to go over that week's readings and have members share about what stood out to them in the lesson. You will then want to go over the questions at the end of the chapter for the rest of your time. If some do not want to share their answers, do not force them. Thank everyone that shares for participating and encourage those that don't. Encourage members to use the Reflection pages at he end of each chapter during the week for journaling and notes. End in prayer.

## SESSION 8—CREATING PERSONAL PLANS OF CHANGE

### Leading the Session:

Go over the group guidelines for respecting participants as they share their plans.

Have participants read action plans aloud.

Have them sign the places provided in their books, committing them to follow the plans of action they have created.

Talk about the specific next steps that they can take (for example, enrolling in a twelve-steps or other recovery program or a personal training or exercise program).

Make sure they have all the resources they need to fulfill their action plans.

Thank them for coming and close in prayer.

Hold hands and sing "Amazing Grace."

## NOTES

**Chapter One**

1. Chip Dodd, *The Voice of the Heart: A Call to Full Living* (Franklin, TN: Sage Hill Resources, 2001).
2. Ibid, 78.
3. George Sheehan, *Personal Best: The Foremost Philosopher of Fitness Shares Techniques and Tactics for Success and Self-Liberation* (New York: Rodale Press, 1992), 30.
4. *Random House Webster's College Dictionary*, s.v. "cynical."
5. Theodore Roosevelt, "Citizenship in a Republic: The Man in the Arena" (speech, Sorbonne, Paris, April 23, 1910), http://www.theodore-roosevelt.com/trsorbonnespeech.html.
6. *Reader's Digest*, October 1991, 62.

**Chapter Two**

1. Chip Dodd, *The Voice of the Heart: A Call to Full Living* (Franklin, TN: Sage Hill Resources, 2001), 67.
2. Melody Beattie, *Codependent No More: How to Stop Controlling Others and Start Caring for Yourself* (New York: HarperCollins, 1992), 53.
3. Tom Rath and Donald Clifton, *How Full is Your Bucket? Positive Strategies for Work and Life* (Princeton, NJ: Gallup Press, 2004), 19.
4. Gerald May, *Addiction and Grace* (San Francisco: HarperSanFrancisco, 1991).
5. Thom Rutledge, *Embracing Fear and Finding the Courage to Live Your Life* (New York, NY: HarperCollins, 2002).

**Chapter Three**

1. John Powell, *A Reason to Live! A Reason to Die!* (Allen, TX: Tabor Pub, 1972).
2. Max Lucado, *Grace for the Moment* (Nashville, TN: Thomas Nelson, 2000).

**Chapter Four**

1. Deuteronomy 31:6.

**Chapter Five**

1. Charles Swindoll, *The Tale of the Tardy Oxcart* (Nashville, TN: W Publishing, 1998), 400.
2. George Sheehan, *Personal Best: The Foremost Philosopher of Fitness Shares Techniques and Tactics for Success and Self-Liberation* (New York: Rodale Press, 1992), 19.
3. Ibid.
4. Ibid, 15.
5. "Memorable quote for *Braveheart*," Internet Movie Database, Inc., http://www.imdb.com/title/tt0112573/quotes.
6. "Maryanne Williamson quotes," Thinkexist.com, http://thinkexist.com/quotation/our-deepest-fear-is-not-that-we-are-inadequate/397505.html.

7. Barbara Slavin, "Professor who 'did not fear death' likely saved students," USA Today, June 15, 2007, http://www.usatoday.com/news/nation/2007-04-17-vt-victims-librescu_n.htm.
8. Peter Shaffer, *Equus* (New York, NY: Penguin), 100.

## Chapter Six

1. At Restore Ministries, we follow the twelve steps in Mike O'Neil's *Power to Choose: Twelve Steps to Wholeness.* If you would like more information about this program or to find one near you, go to www.restoreymca.org.